The Happiness Sprinkling Project:
Sets of Signs pass from
Happiness Ambassador to
Happiness Ambassador,
Sprinkling Happiness in towns
and cities all over the country
and beyond.
Come Sprinkle with us!

Please invest
in Happiness:

HappinessSprinklingProject.org

YOU ARE AWESOME

YOU SPRINKLE HAPPINESS!

Laura Lavigne

TreeHouse Publishing
Anacortes, WA

WHEN WE ARE BORN
— OR MAYBE A LITTLE BIT BEFORE —
WE GET A GIFT.

WE ALL GET A GIFT.
THE SAME ONE.

YOU GET ONE, YOUR MOM GETS ONE,
THE MAILMAN GETS ONE,
TEACHERS AND BOSSES GET ONE.

THE LADY WHO PACKS YOUR
GROCERIES AT THE STORE?
SHE GETS ONE TOO.

THE EXACT SAME GIFT.

THE GIFT IS WAY COOL.

IT'S ACTUALLY

A SUPER POWER.

OUR SUPER POWER
IS NOT
TO FLY.

IT'S MUCH COOLER
THAN THAT.

OUR SUPER POWER
IS NOT
TO BECOME INVISIBLE.

IN FACT, IT IS JUST ABOUT THE COOLEST
SUPER POWER
THERE COULD BE.

OUR SUPER POWER IS:

THE POWER TO SPRINKLE PEOPLE WITH HAPPINESS.

LET'S SAY IT AGAIN.

OUR SUPER POWER IS:

THE POWER TO SPRINKLE PEOPLE WITH HAPPINESS.

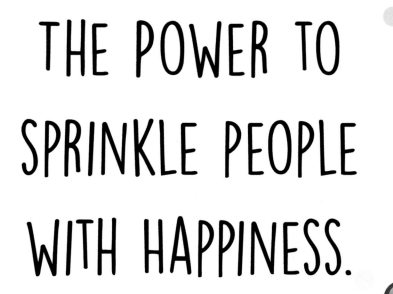

OUR SUPER POWER
TO SPRINKLE PEOPLE
WITH HAPPINESS
MEANS THAT WHEN WE ARE
AROUND THEM ...

... PEOPLE MAY
FEEL A LITTLE
HAPPIER.

OR MORE LOVED.

OR BRAVER.

OR MAYBE A
LITTLE SMARTER.

OR A LITTLE BIT
MORE BEAUTIFUL

SOMETIMES WE DO THIS BY USING
OUR SMILE,
AND NOT VERY MANY WORDS.

SOMETIMES WE DO THIS BY USING
JUST THE SMILE THAT LIVES
IN OUR EYES.

SOMETIMES WE DO THIS BY USING
OUR WORDS.

WORDS FROM OUR MOUTHS,
OR WORDS ON PAPER.

OR OUR HUGS.

OR BY JUST SITTING NEXT TO
SOMEONE,
AND NOT TALKING.

USING OUR SUPER POWER
REALLY QUIETLY.

THERE ARE SO MANY WAYS TO USE
THE POWER TO SPRINKLE PEOPLE
WITH HAPPINESS...

... SO MANY WAYS THAT NO ONE
HAS FOUND ALL OF THEM YET.

(MAYBE YOU

WILL FIND A NEW WAY?)

NOW I MUST TELL YOU SOMETHING.

SOMETIMES,
WE MAY NOT FEEL LIKE USING
OUR SUPER POWER,
ESPECIALLY WHEN WE ARE A LITTLE HURT.

AND THEN, INSTEAD OF SPRINKLING HAPPINESS,
WE MAY DECIDE TO USE A DIFFERENT POWER.

ONE THAT HAS SUCH A SAD NAME THAT
NO ONE HAS EVER BEEN ABLE
TO SAY IT OUT LOUD.

WHEN WE USE THAT
OTHER POWER,
WE CAN MAKE PEOPLE
FEEL BAD.

OR FEEL SMALL,
AND NOT GOOD ABOUT
THEMSELVES.

OR NOT LOVED.

SOMETIMES WE DO THIS BY PUTTING
SOME MEANNESS IN OUR EYES.

SOMETIMES WE DO IT BY USING OUR WORDS,
OR OUR TOUCH.

OR EVEN OUR THOUGHTS.

WHEN WE CHOOSE TO DO THAT (WHICH WE ALMOST
ALL DO SOMETIMES), IT'S NOT AT ALL AS MUCH FUN
AS USING OUR SUPER POWER TO SPRINKLE HAPPINESS.

OH...

ONE MORE THING ABOUT OUR

SUPER POWER

TO SPRINKLE

HAPPINESS:

WE NEVER NEED TO REMEMBER TO TAKE IT WITH US
WHEN WE LEAVE THE HOUSE.

BECAUSE IT ALWAYS JUMPS IN OUR POCKET,
AND IT GOES WITH US EVERYWHERE WE GO.

AND IT NEVER RUNS OUT OF
BATTERIES.

OR GETS BROKEN.

OR TIRED.
OR GRUMPY.

IT'S ALWAYS READY,

AND IT'S ALWAYS FREE.

ALL WE HAVE TO DO IS

REMEMBER TO USE IT.

AND GUESS WHAT?
HERE IS ONE LAST PIECE OF MAGIC:

EVERY TIME YOU CHOOSE TO USE YOUR SUPER
POWER TO MAKE SOMEONE FEEL A LITTLE
HAPPIER, A LITTLE MORE BEAUTIFUL, A LITTLE
BRAVER OR MORE LOVED,

YOU GET SPRINKLED, TOO!

WHEN THAT HAPPENS, YOU FEEL
A LITTLE HAPPIER.

A LITTLE MORE BEAUTIFUL.

A LITTLE BRAVER.

I AM SO

HAPPY

THAT WE ALL

HAVE

THIS POWER.

THE POWER TO
SPRINKLE PEOPLE
WITH HAPPINESS.

I AM SO HAPPY THAT...

...YOU ARE
A HAPPINESS SPRINKLER!

DEDICATED TO ALL THE HAPPINESS SPRINKLERS OF THE WORLD.
YOU ROCK!

First edition 2015

ISBN-13: 978-0692556795
ISBN-10: 0692556796

Printed in the USA

This book was written and illustrated by Laura Lavigne
TreeHouse Publishing
619 Commercial Avenue . The Ballroom
Anacortes, WA 98221
lauralavigne.com

Please invest
in Happiness:

HappinessSprinklingProject.org